# NAILSEA AND D FOOTPATH

### AN EASY TO USE MAP FOR WALKERS
### IN BOOK FORM

### COVERING AN AREA OF 96 SQUARE KILOMETRES
### WITH NAILSEA AT THE CENTRE

### THIS AREA HAS A VERY EXTENSIVE NETWORK
### OF WELL USED RIGHTS OF WAY

### THE MAPS ARE HAND DRAWN
### TO AN APPROX SCALE OF
### 1: 12500

### BASED ON ORDNANCE SURVEY 1:25000 MAPS
### WITH AMENDMENTS ARISING FROM A SURVEY
### ON FOOT OF EACH PUBLIC RIGHT OF WAY
### COMPLETED BY
### MEMBERS AND FRIENDS OF
### NAILSEA AND DISTRICT FOOTPATH GROUP

### EIGHT LOCAL CIRCULAR WALKS
### WITH EASY TO FOLLOW INSTRUCTIONS
### ARE INCLUDED

Maps reproduced by permission of Ordnance Survey on behalf of HMSO
© 2010. All rights reserved. Ordnance Survey licence number 100049647.

# CONTENTS

**Map Symbols and Cautions**
　　　　　　Front and Back　　　　　　　　Inside cover

**WALK 1**　　Library, Jacklands,
　　　　　　Towerhouse Woods.　　3 miles　　Page 1

**WALK 2**　　Pound Lane, Tickenham Court,
　　　　　　Cadbury Camp Lane,
　　　　　　Stonedge Batch.　　5 miles　　Pages 2 & 3

**WALK 3**　　East End, Backwell Common,
　　　　　　The Elms.　　4 ½ miles　　Pages 4 & 5

**WALK 4**　　Cradle Bridge, Sidelands Cottage,
　　　　　　Truckle Wood, Flax Bourton.
　　　　　　　　　　　　6 miles　　Pages 6 & 7

**WALK 5**　　Trendlewoods, Backwell Playing Fields,
　　　　　　Backwell Church, Cherry Wood,
　　　　　　Backwell Common　　5 ½ miles　　Pages 8 & 9

**MAP KEY**　　Map Page Positions　　　　　Pages 10 & 11

**MAPS**　　96 SQ KM Centred on Nailsea　　Pages 12 to 43

**WALK 6**　　Hannah More Road, Grove School,
　　　　　　Youngwood Lane, South Common,
　　　　　　Nurse Batch.　　3 ½ miles　　Pages 44 & 45

**WALK 7**　　Backwell Lake, Nailsea Ponds,
　　　　　　Backwell Common.　　5 ¼ miles　　Pages 46 & 47

**WALK 8**　　Linear Park, Parish Brook, North
　　　　　　Lane, Kingshill.　　2 ¾ miles　　Pages 48 & 49

## WALK 1   3 miles

## Library, Jacklands, Tower House Woods
*A pleasant walk up through woods, with views across Nailsea.*

From the library go past the church along Christ Church Close and then along Silver Street to just past the Methodist Church and turn right, cross Westway and continue ahead (North). Turn right at children's play area through linear park to Clevedon Road. Cross road into Greenfield Crescent and after about 150 yds. turn left into playing field. Turn left again behind houses, over stile and right (North) alongside hedge.

At end of field cross the footbridge and continue in same direction between fish ponds. Cross drive to Fish Farm and continue through to private road and turn left to Clevedon Road. Bear right along pavement for about 100yds then turn right up drive near old quarry. Follow drive up and around to right at top, then along path to stone stile. Over stile, turn left for a few feet then right, along drive away from house. Continue straight ahead ignoring where the drive turns away to your left and follow path through the woods.

At Y junction in tracks continue left, slightly uphill, ignoring right hand, slightly downhill route. At path junction just before bungalow on right, turn right, downhill. At the bottom of hill over stile into field. Continue straight ahead (South) across field and stream towards second stream. At second stream turn right and follow path with stream on your left. Continue to the next footbridge which you crossed earlier. Cross and return alongside hedge to Geenfield Crescent via stile and playing field, as before. Turn right to Clevedon Road then left along footpath on left of road, crossing Southfield Road and Heathfield Road. Cross Clevedon Road into car park, bear left and take the underpass to the precinct and return to the Library.

## WALK 2    5 miles

### Pound Lane, Tickenham Court, Cadbury Camp Lane, Stonedge Batch

*A more strenuous walk with a climb over Tickenham Ridge and back, but well worth it for the views. The walk could be shortened by starting from Tickenham Church and walking back over Causeway bridge to first stile and gate on right.*

From Pound Lane with the junction with Fryth Way take walkway in WSW direction for 40 yards to path junction and grass triangle. Bear left on walking for 80 yards passing next grass triangle on left and continue to junction. Turn right, then left onto Causeway View, cross over and, after about 50 yards, take footpath between houses and over stile into field. Cross field to gate opposite and cross stream. Turn left to follow stream to Causeway.

Turn right along Causeway towards Tickenham Church for about 450 yards, crossing bridge over stream, then left at gate and stile just before bend in road.  Follow the base of the slope with stone wall above on right and then follow stream on right for about 440 yards through gate and cross stream at stone bridge. Continue ahead, North, across field to reach bridge over river. Cross bridge and stile into field. Bear slightly right across field to stile. Over stile and along passageway to a drive and road B3103.

Cross road and turn left for a few yards to a pedestrian gate and path. Follow this path to a stile and bear left on path with hill on right to another stile.

Again bear left along permissive path to next stile then turn sharp right uphill to more stiles leading to track (Cadbury Camp Lane). Turn right here for about 50 yards then left along path downhill under motorway viaduct to tarmac lane.

Turn right along this lane for about 300 yards then turn right uphill on bridleway and under motorway viaduct. Near top of slope on left, at junction with path to left, look for memorial plaque to Dennis Thomas, a founder member of Gordano Footpath Group and committee member of Nailsea and District Footpath Group.

Continue on bridleway to Cadbury Camp Lane. Left along lane for about 3/4 of a mile to find a low, ladder type, stile on right next to 'South Fall'. Over stile follow path steeply downhill then bear right through wood to reach a bridle path at edge of wood. Over the stile here, on clear days, there are excellent views towards Nailsea, Cleeve and Weston.

Bear slightly right downhill aiming for right corner of wood. From here bear slightly right again towards gate and stile. Continue in same direction across corner of next field to gate and stile on left. Turn slightly left across next field to gate and stile. Continue in same direction across next field to gate and stile in corner and to main road (B3128). Turn right along road to junction then right again, **take care there is no pavement**, for about 25 yards. Cross with care and continue for a few more yards to stone stile and footpath sign on left. Over stile turn left and head south through two gates and over two stiles. Over last stile turn right down slope and cross bridge.

(If you started at Tickenham Church turn right along river bank to lane, then left along lane to Church)

Continue in same direction down slope from bridge to another bridge over rhyne. Cross rhyne then bear right towards pylon and cross next rhyne over bridge. Continue diagonally right to top corner of field. Right through gate then take first gate opening on left. Cross the field passing electricity pylon, over stile and across narrow field to further stile leading to passageway and Goodwin Drive. Cross over and take walkway just to right through to Pound Lane. Turn right to the start point.

## WALK 3    4 ½ miles

**East End, Backwell Common, The Elms**
*A fairly level walk using several surfaced walkways and some field paths.*

From Nailsea Library go down steps and through to Crown Glass Square, past Britannia Building Society and cross Stockway south using pedestrian lights and along walkway to Valley Gardens.

Bear left up Valley Gardens then turn right along Hillcrest road and a few yards along Coombe Road. Then left along walkway and under Mizzymead Road continuing on Ash Hayes Drive. Turn left on walkway between Nos. 58 and 59 then past Nailsea School playing fields.

At Ash Hayes Road cross and turn left. Cross Station Road taking path to the right of Trendlewood Cottage and into Trendlewoods. Continue on track, through pedestrian gate, past disused quarry and bear right on tarmac walkway alongside playing fields to far end and on to Avening Close. Cross Trendlewood Way and follow walkway East to junction.

Turn left on walkway and cross Bucklands View. After about 100 yards bear right on walkway and keep right, passing between wooden fences to far end. Turn left on open space for about 75 yards then cross over then cross stream using small footbridge on your right then along left hand side of field.

# 5

Left through gateway and immediately right to follow hedges to road (Backwell Common).

Turn left on road to far end of row of Houses (Russetts Cottages) on your right. Turn right along road for 20 yards then left along Cider Farm drive. Just before the farm buildings turn left on through a gateway and across three fields to reach stile at bend in road.

Cross road slightly left and through gate following hedge on right to next gate. Through this gate then turn left and follow hedge on left passing old farm buildings to reach stile and footbridge on left. Cross footbridge and turn right to cross field.

At far side of field turn sharp left onto footpath heading North West towards stile. Continue in next field past electricity pole to gateway. Do not exit to road but turn right to follow footpath to river as it skirts Brook Farm. Bear left to follow river halfway across triangular field then bear slightly left to stile. Continue west across next field to gate.

Turn right before gate and follow hedge along footpath through two fields then over stile and bear slightly left to stile and footbridge. Continue west up field to track and on to Children's Play Area, proceed towards top corner and leave through walkway turning left then right (Elm Lodge Lane) and onto Lodge Lane. Turn left to junction with Trendlewood Way, cross and proceed for a few yards then along open space on right crossing Hawthorn Way and Nailsea Park (road).

Continue through Scotch Horn Park on walkway passing old Winding Tower. Go round the Scotch Horn Centre, cross the car park and enter passageway to the right of Brockway Medical Centre. Take left fork to High Street and continue to precinct and Library.

## WALK 4    6 miles

## Cradle Bridge, Sidelands Cottage, Truckle Wood
*A walk across fields up through Wraxall with views across Nailsea then some woodlands and finally alongside a river.*

Starting from the roundabout at the junction of Lodge Lane and High Street, go through gap in wall and keep to hedge on left. Just past garage bear right across grass, keeping a small round copse on the right, then take path between two copses to stile. Right along hedge to metal gate, then diagonally left across field to opposite corner and cross river via a footbridge. Go through gate opposite, across track. Bear right towards a curve in the hedge, and follow this hedge to a gate on right. Go through this gate then immediately left keeping, the hedge on your left. At the corner go over stile, then immediately left over another stile. Now go diagonally right up hill towards a grey, stone house at the top of the field.

Cross main road and go up steps into field. Bear right uphill, crossing a wooden fence, and continue on diagonally to right-hand corner at top of field. Over stile, through trees for a short distance, then turn left to follow a track through woods, and on between the buildings at Rectory Cottage. Continue on gravel track to just before it emerges onto Wraxall Hill road, then turn right onto track which winds up through the woods. Veer right at a sunken 3-way junction and continue on broad path to top Go over a stile and straight ahead through field, passing Sidelands cottages on left. At end of field turn right along field edge, keeping stone wall on left. Go over stile and down through wood to stile in boundary wall on left. Over stile, then immediately right down hill to private road. Take path opposite down through woods. Continue through woods, crossing a broad track which leads down to field on right.

At end of wood, turn right down a broad track, and then between two houses onto the B3130.

Cross road, over a stile then head downhill to another stile. Turn right along track towards Watercress Farm. Where track forks, go left to pass in front of farm house, then straight on between a small building on left and converted barn on right to gate in fence straight ahead. Bear left across field to far corner. Turn right along track.

In a short distance take gate on left and follow path round Gable Farm. Just before gate onto road, go through gate on right then bear right to gap in centre of hedge on far side of field. Bear right across next field to far corner. Go straight ahead across centre of next field, aiming for masts on skyline on Dundry Hill. Through gap in hedge, then bear slightly right to metal gate in front of low buildings. Turn right and follow road. Just past railway bridge, turn right onto cycleway.

Continue along cycleway until it turns right over the railway. Cross bridge then leave cycleway and continue straight ahead along a grassy track between two hedges. Where path turns sharply to right, go over stile on left then diagonally right across centre of field to metal gate in far corner. Go over stile by gate into field, then aim for the right-hand end of the building ahead (Watercress Farm). Cross bridge over stream then through gate to front of farm. Turn left past farm buildings then over stile into field.

Go round left-hand edge of field with river on left. At end of wood, through gate and continue with river on left. Ignore footbridge just before Brook Farm and cross second bridge just past farm. Go diagonally across field to stile by oak tree. Cross field to metal gate. Do not go through, but turn right, keeping hedge on left, then over stile at end of field. Continue with hedge on left. In about 100 m go over stile in hedge on left.

Go round left-side of field, with hedge on left, and after about 200 m cross wooden bridge in hedge on left. In a few metres bear right onto broad track. At broad grassy area continue straight ahead through gap in hedge, then take track which curves across centre of field back to start.

## WALK 5    5 ½ miles

## Trendlewoods, Backwell Playing Fields, Backwell Church, Cherry Wood and Backwell Common
*A mainly gentle walk through woods and fields passing Backwell church*

From Scotch Horn Centre go along left side of building and take path on right past circular rose garden to emerge between houses on Scotch Horn Way. Turn left and take walkway between houses, turn right at road and take walkway on left through to Horwood Road and on to Station Road. Cross over, turn right and turn left at first footpath into Trendlewoods.

Follow the path as it turns right by an old quarry. Continue turning right onto a tarmac walkway. Keep bearing right onto Avening Close. Cross Trendlewood Way and follow walkway opposite to junction. Turn right and follow walkway, crossing road. Turn left between houses 15 & 16. Go over stile and turn right, following stream for about 100 yards. Bear left across the field, through gateway towards the railway. Go over stile and through the archway, turn right to emerge by the traffic lights.

**BE VERY CAREFUL - THIS IS A BLIND SPOT**.

Cross road and turn left in front of petrol station. Turn right into Moor Lane. Follow lane past all houses and on to track to reach stile on left. Over stile and follow field boundary to kissing gate. Follow tarmac path to stile, turn right and cross field to kissing gate and sports field. Continue diagonally across field to gate, turn right and follow road around to A370. Cross road and turn left and continue past Ettrick Garage to turn right by The Red Cross building following path through to Church Lane.

Turn left along road to T junction. Turn right along Dark Lane past School and Church to turn right up path beside Court Farm. Follow this path up through the woods until you reach a gate and stile at the top.

Follow the track down the slope to a gate. Through the gate and follow track on left along gulley to a stile. Over stile to lane then right between houses to pass Backwell Club and continue on to A370. Cross road and follow track to left of The George pub by Fairfield Mead to allotments.

At far end of allotments bear right over stile and immediately left on track. Go through gate and then left through field to gate. Through gate turn right and continue through 4 fields and under a railway arch. Continue along a gravel drive onto Backwell Common (road).

Over stile opposite Russett's Cottage across field and through a narrow garden via stiles. Cut across to stile in hedge on right. Cross stream and bear left to follow hedge to next footbridge over stream.

Cross and continue up path opposite between houses into Crewkerne Close. Up Close to Vynes Way. Follow Vynes Way to the left and then bear right uphill past Vynes Close to turn right down Cleeve place for a few yards. turn left up path between houses through to Trendlewood Way.

Cross and continue along Cherington Road, then bear right along Cerney Gardens to end. Continue along short path between houses to path T junction.

Turn right here and almost immediately left along bridleway to pass Golden Valley Vets and School on left. Cross main road at crossing into Millennium Park and back to Scotch Horn Centre.

# MAP KEY

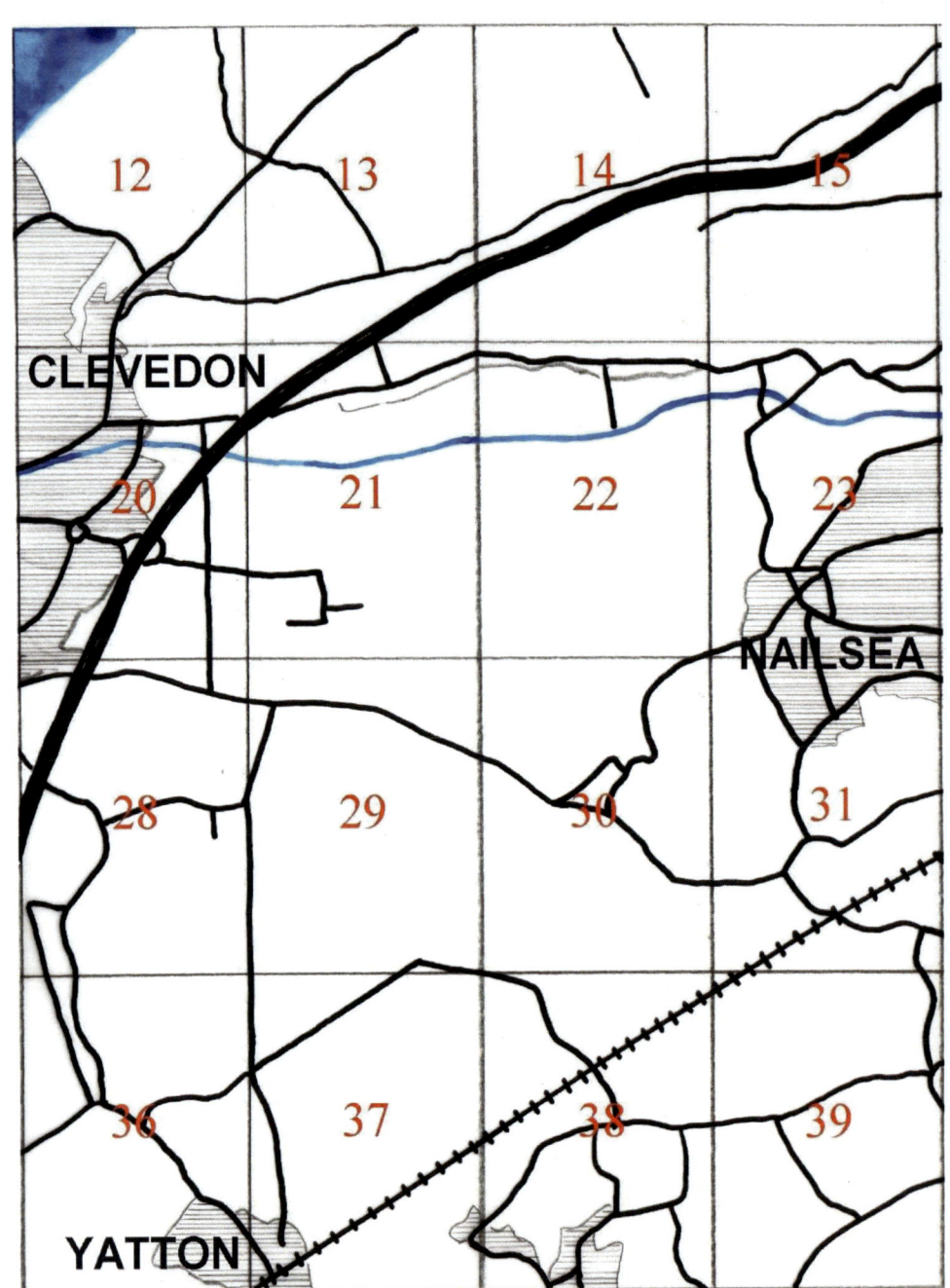

**MAP KEY**

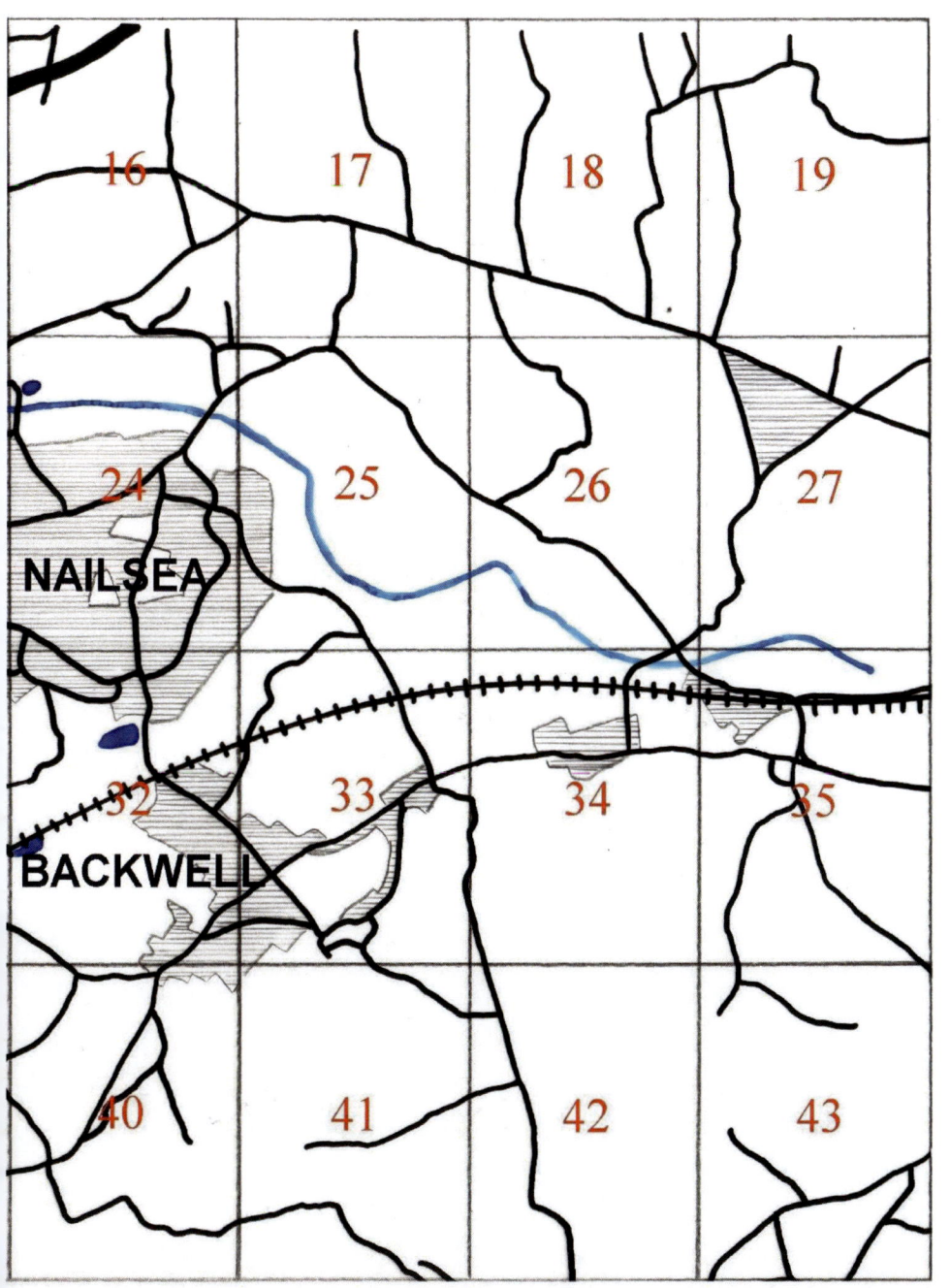

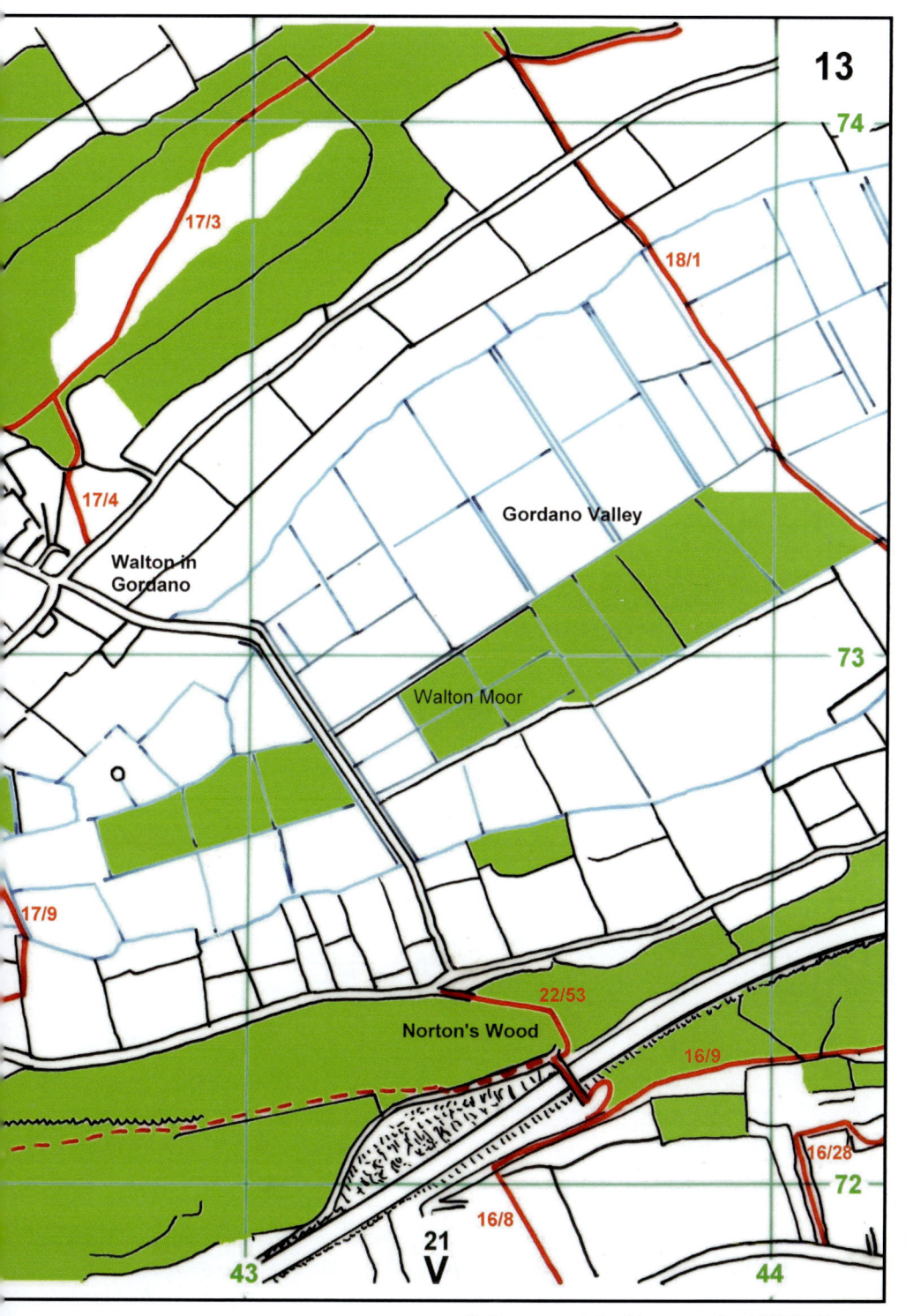

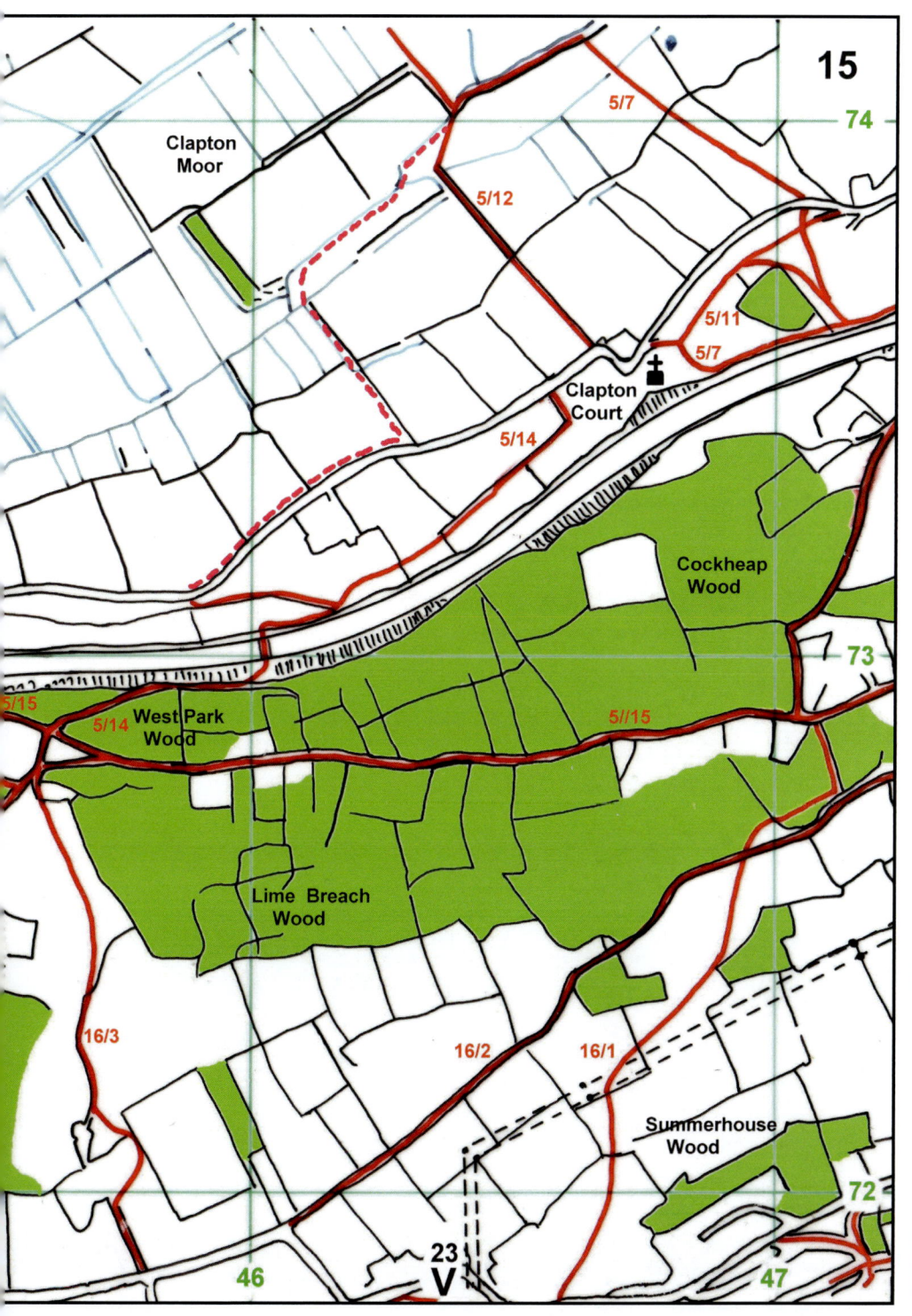

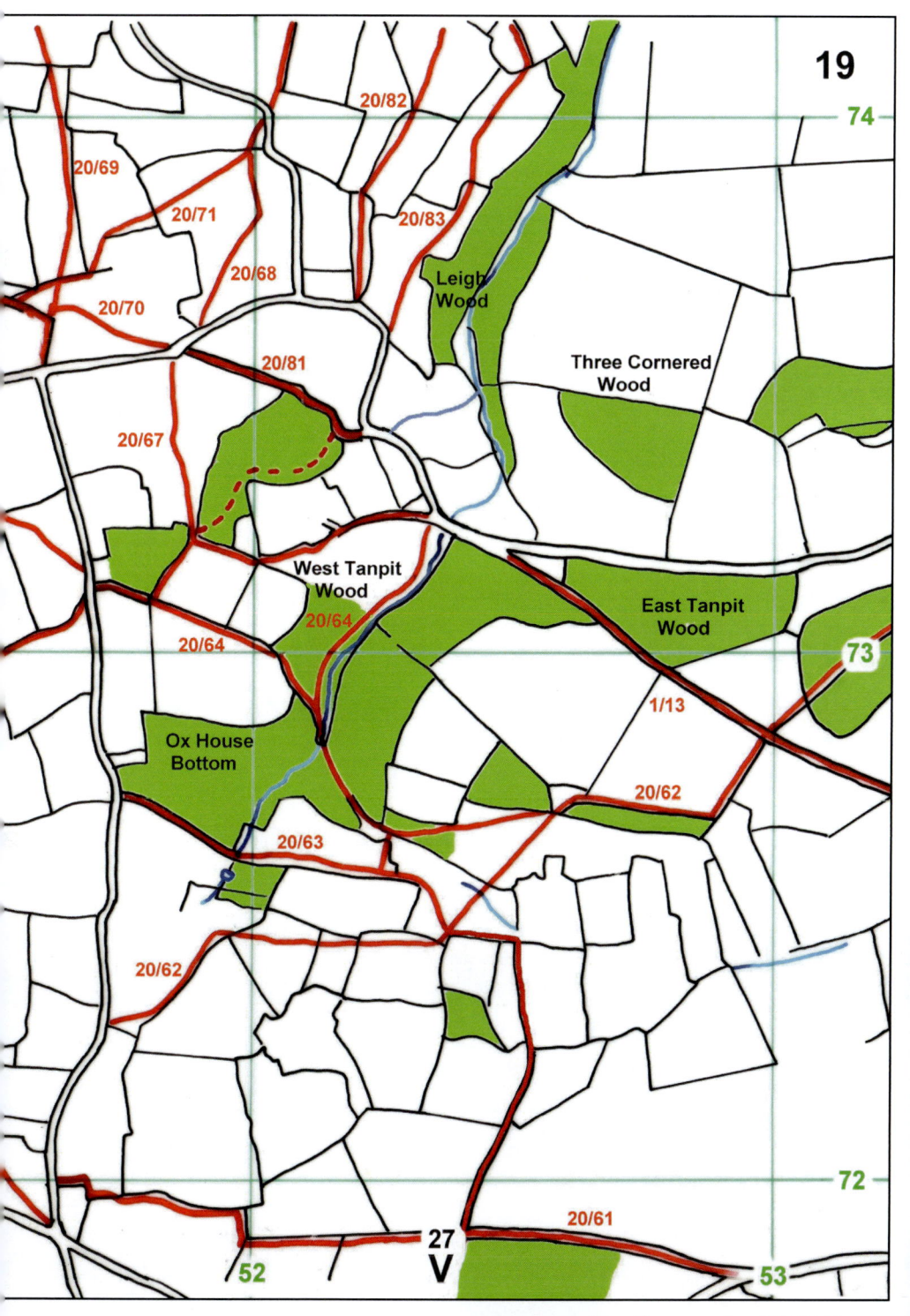

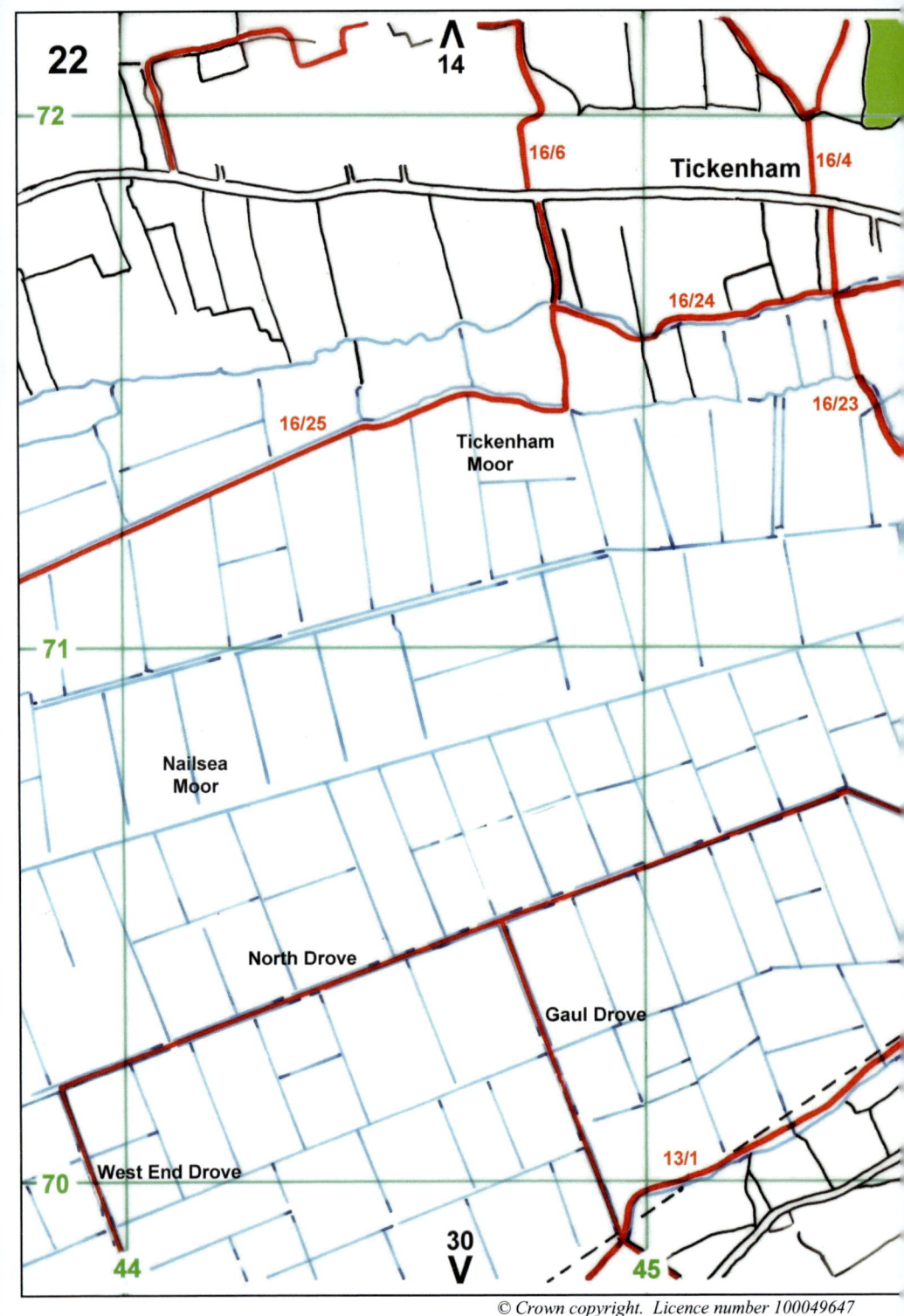

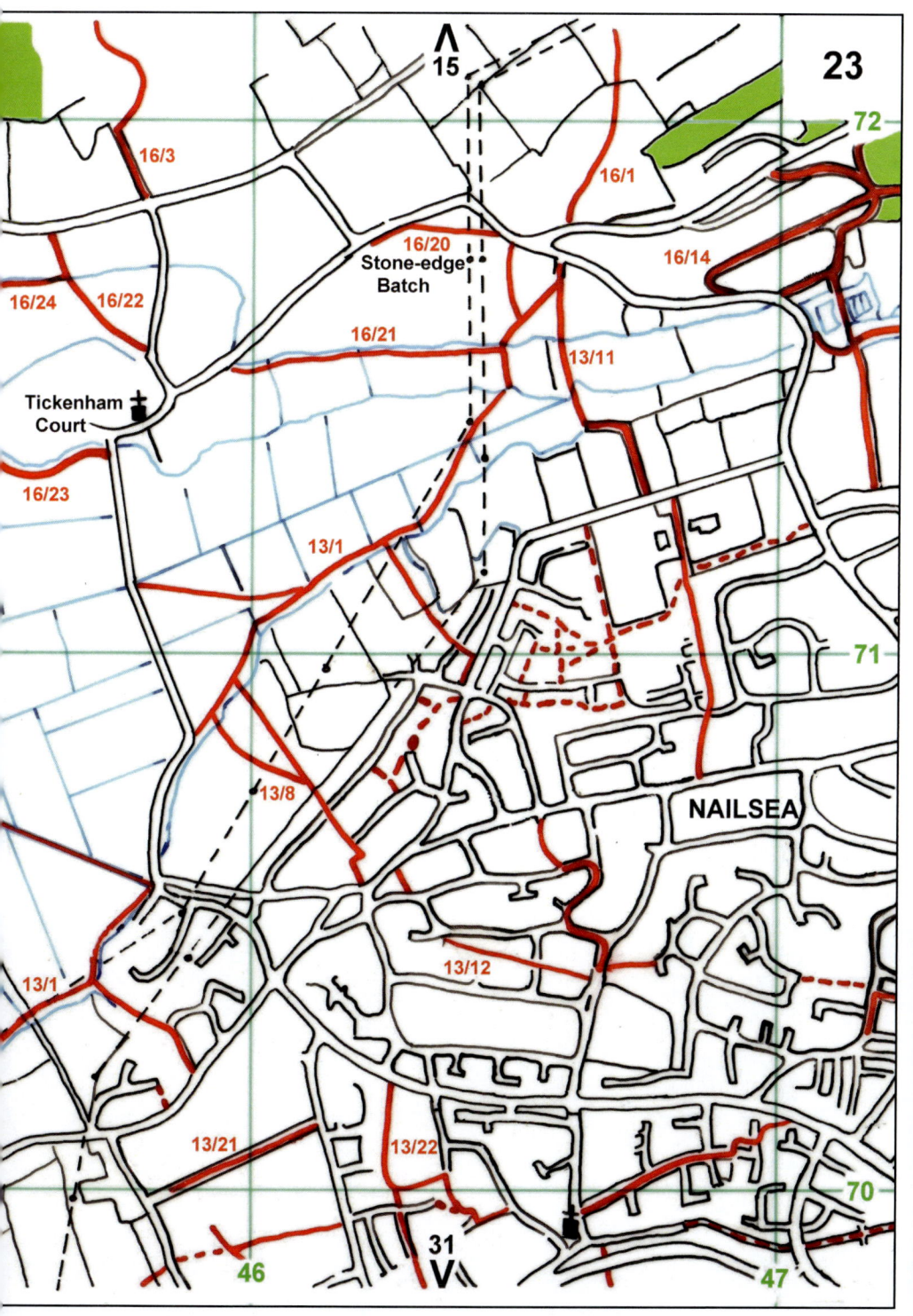

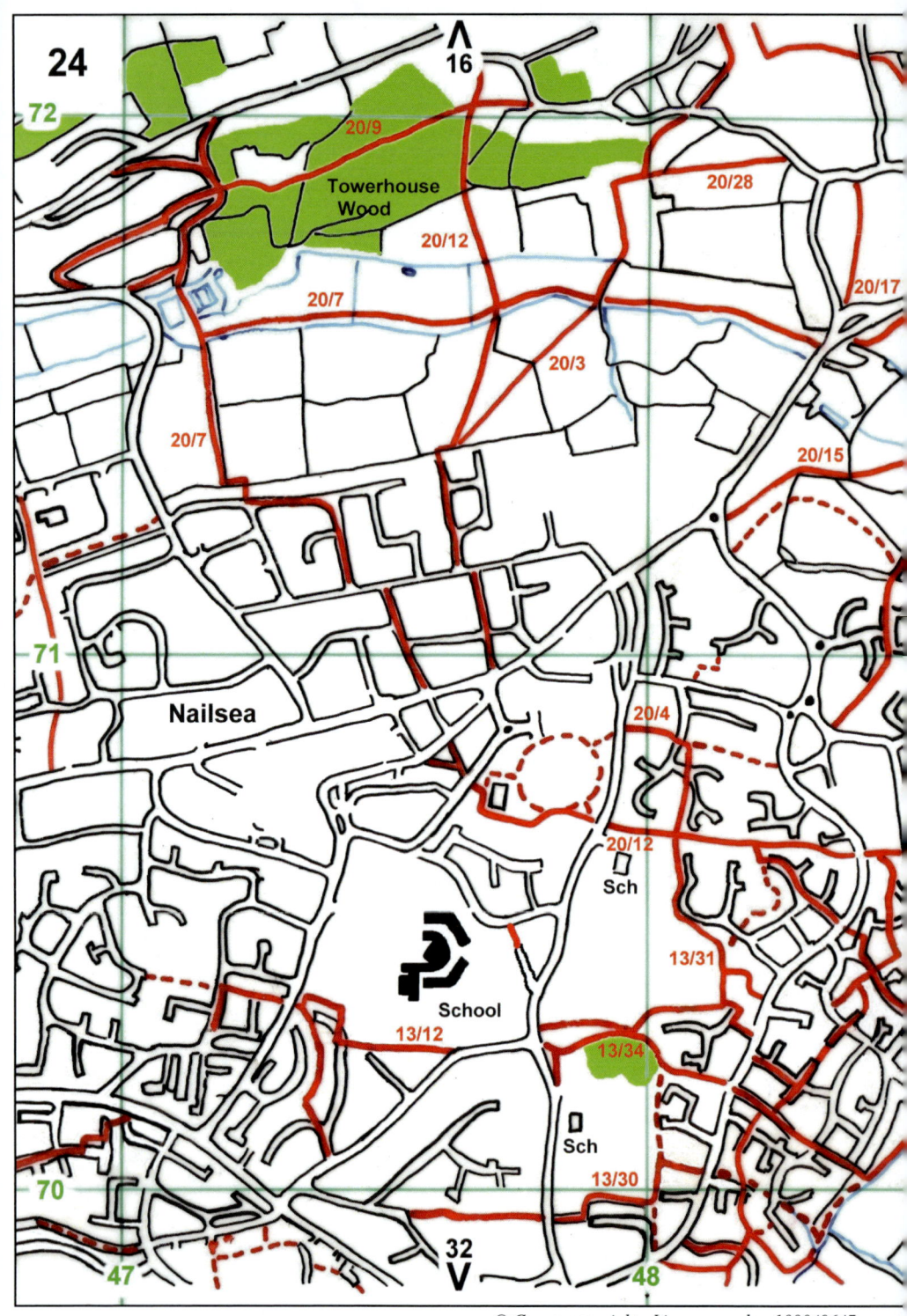

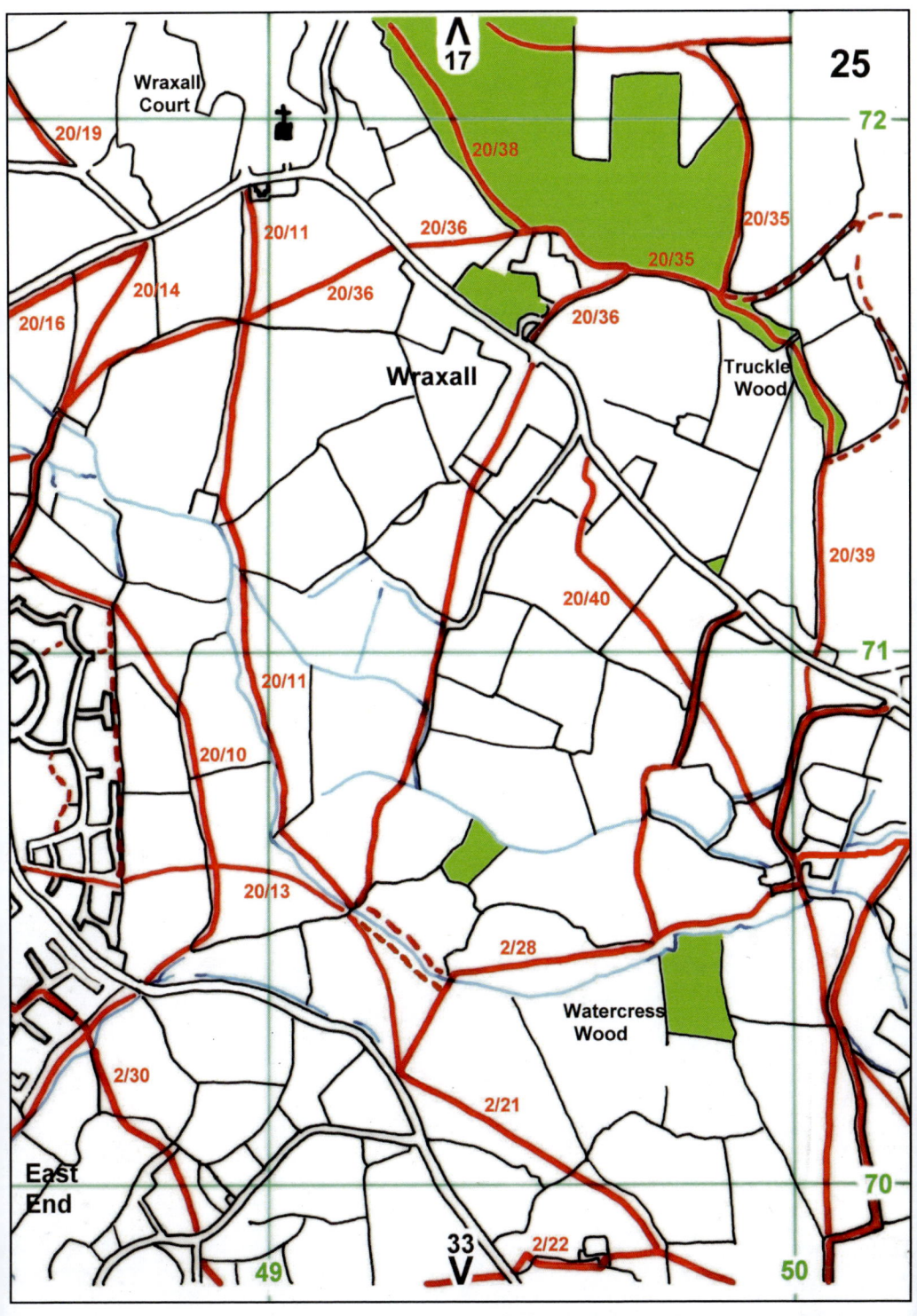

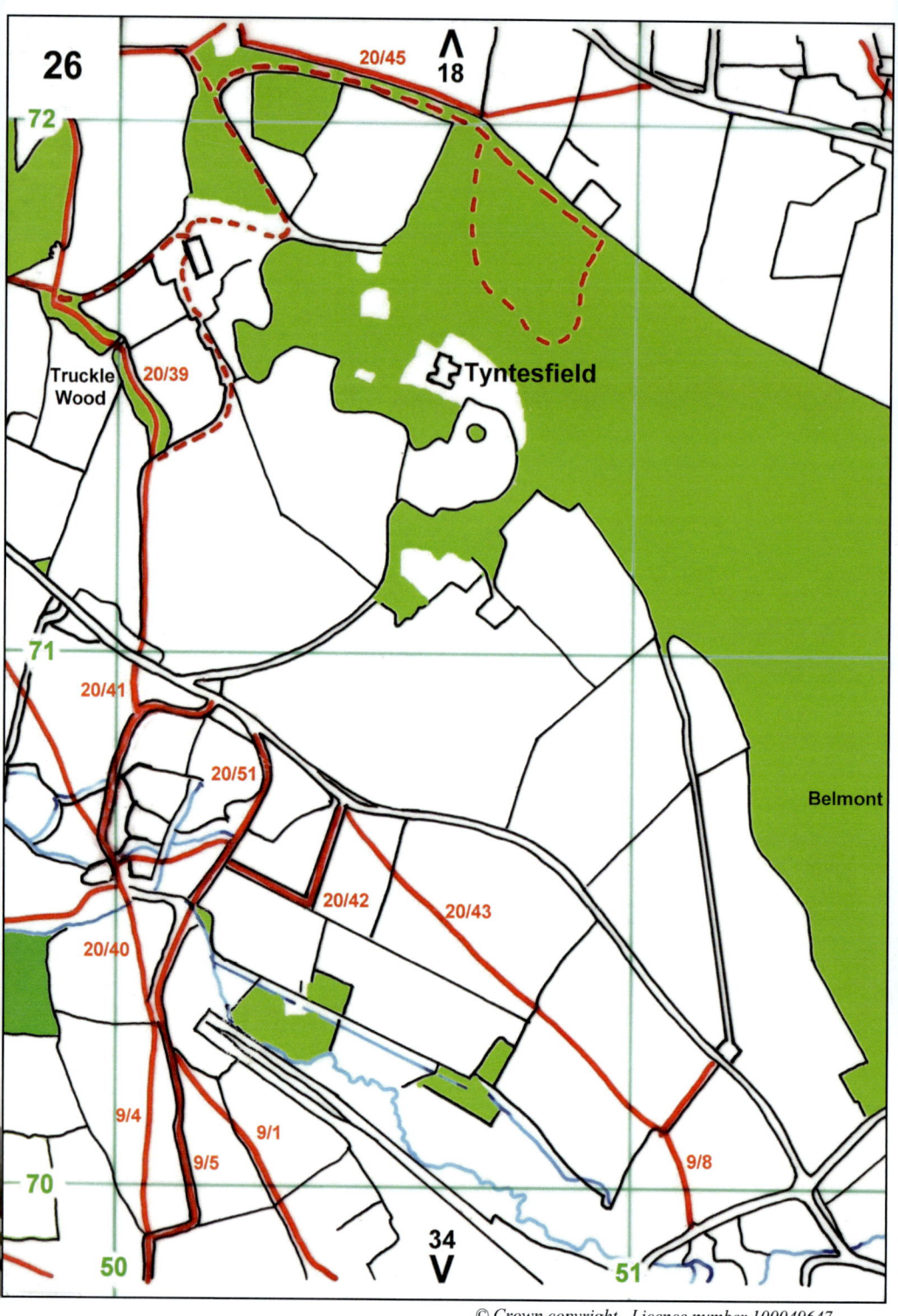

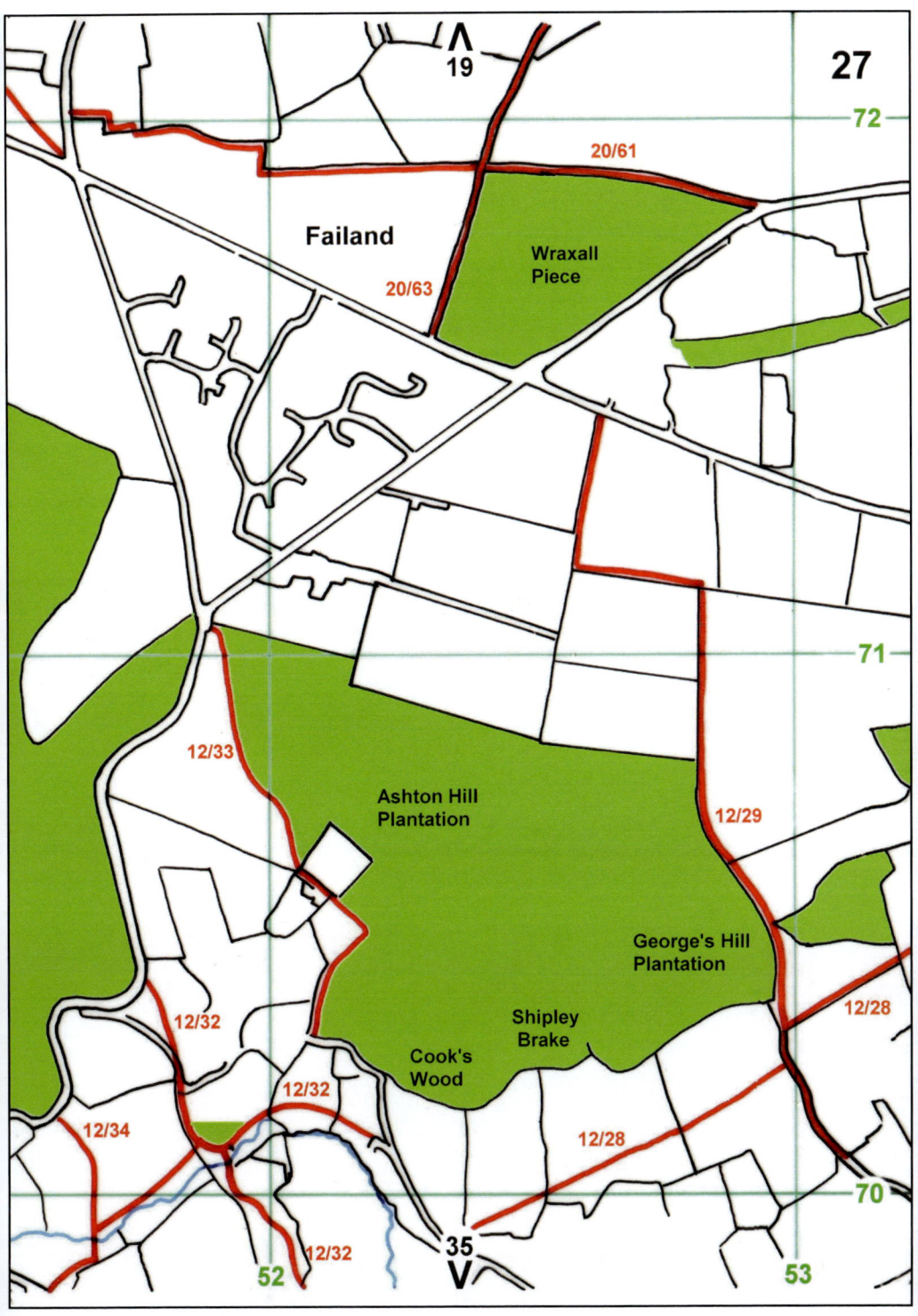

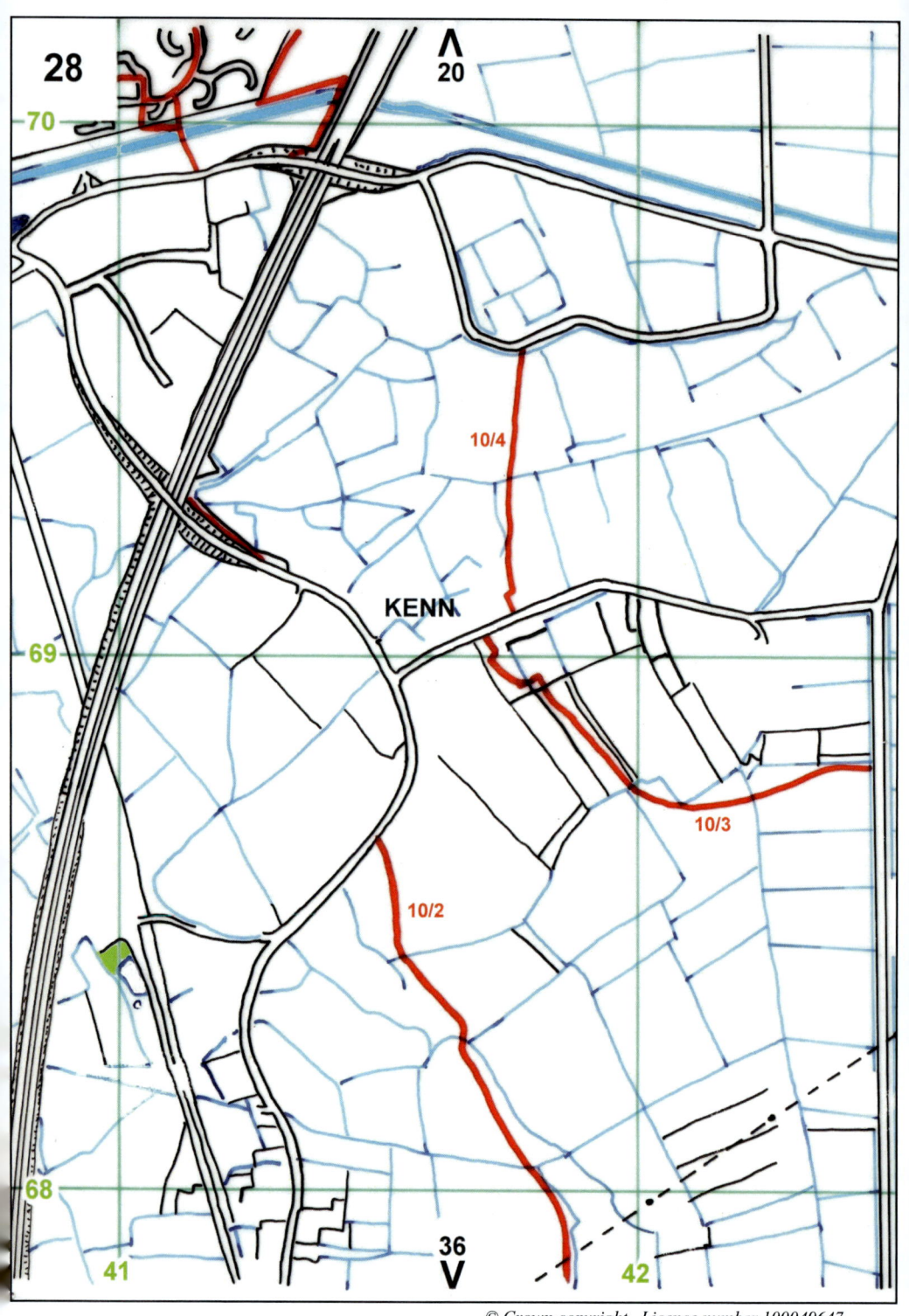

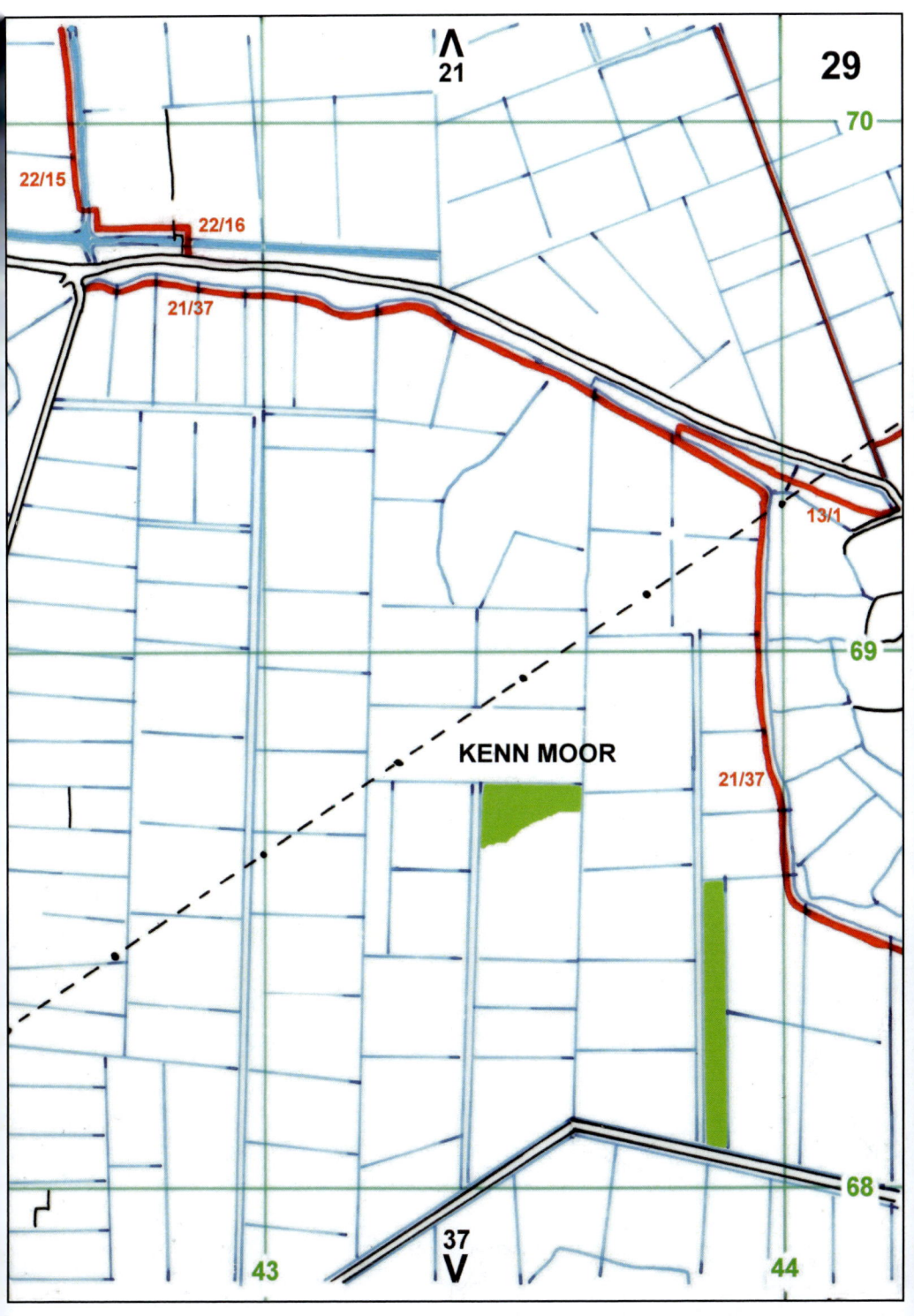

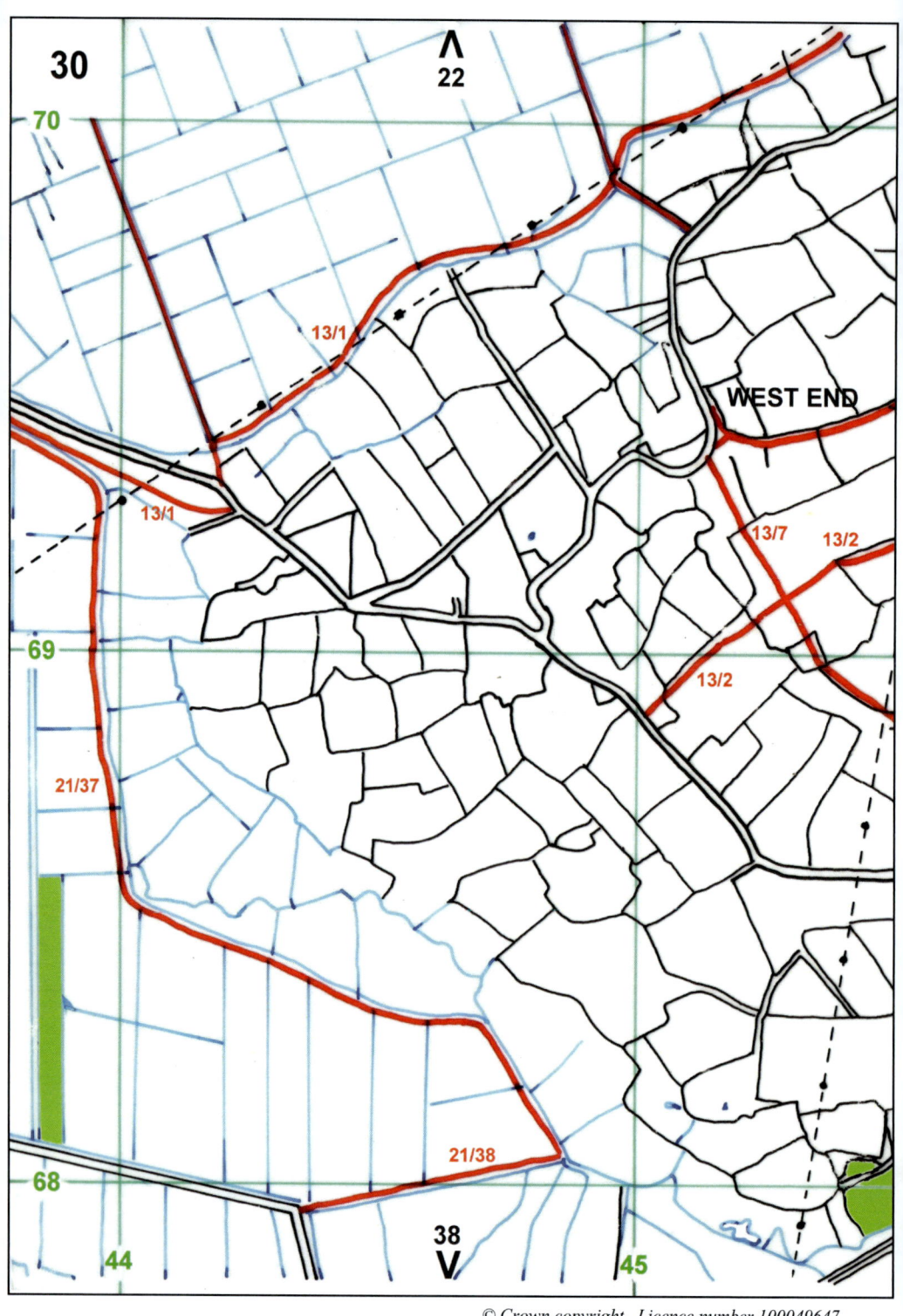

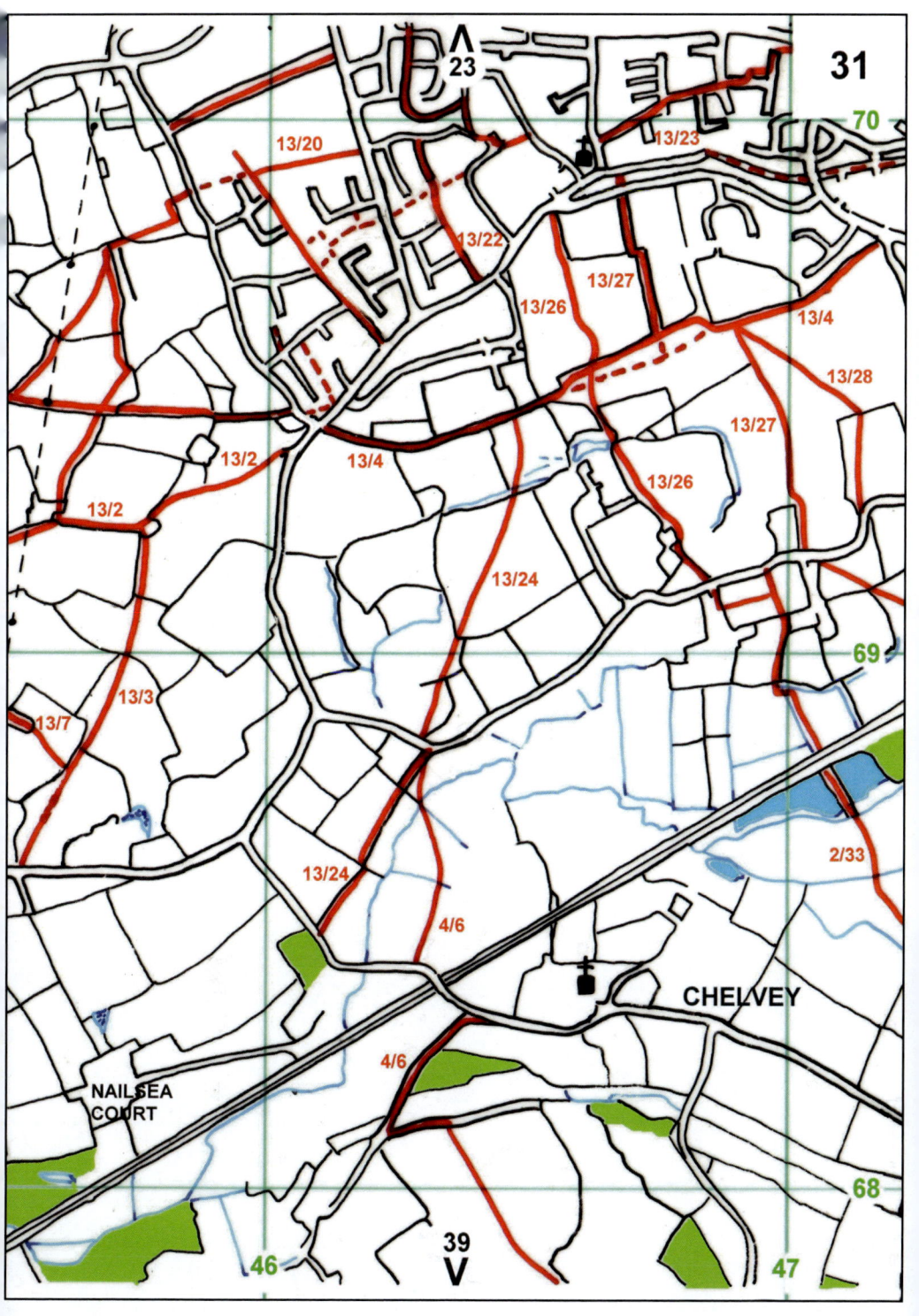

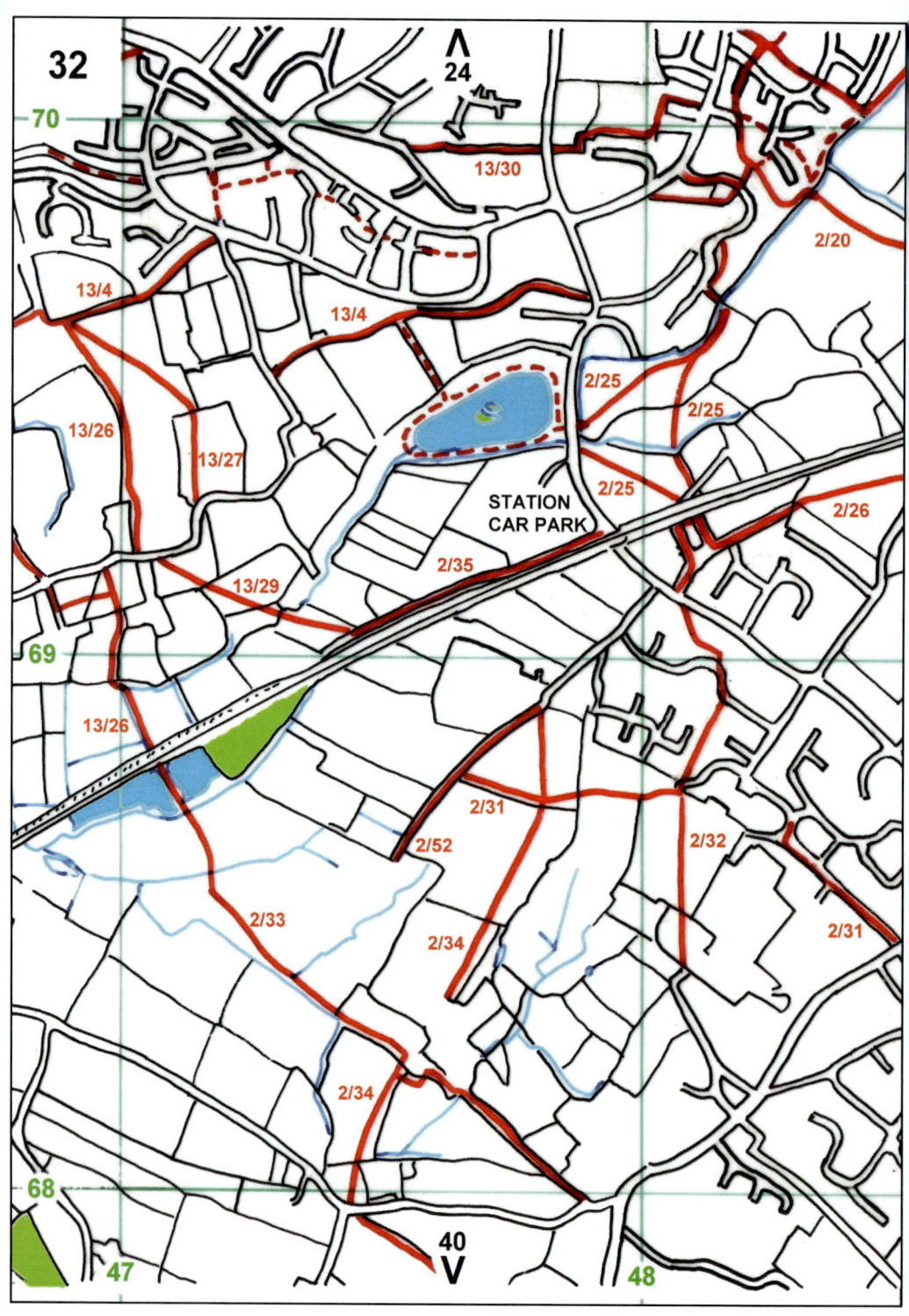

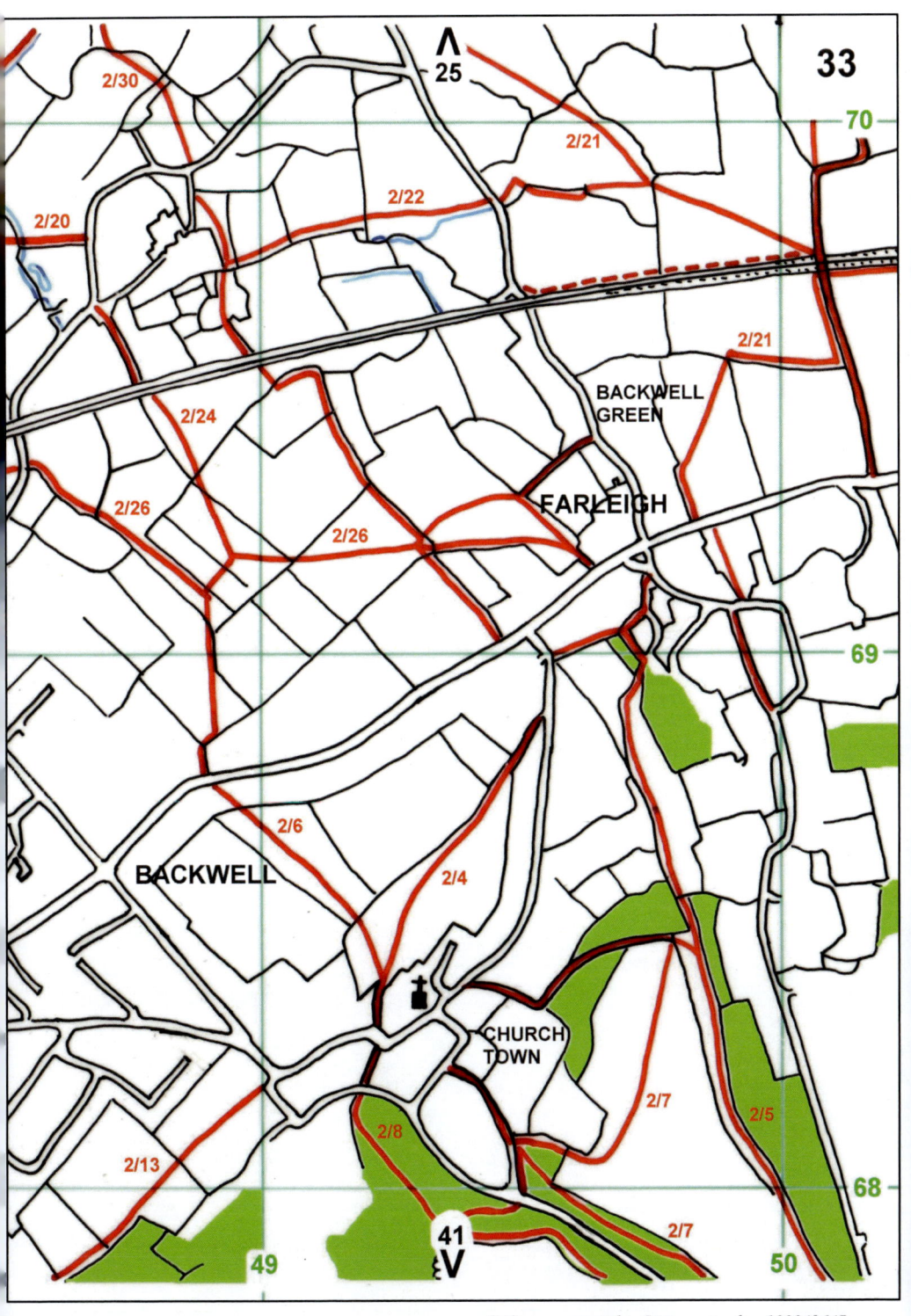

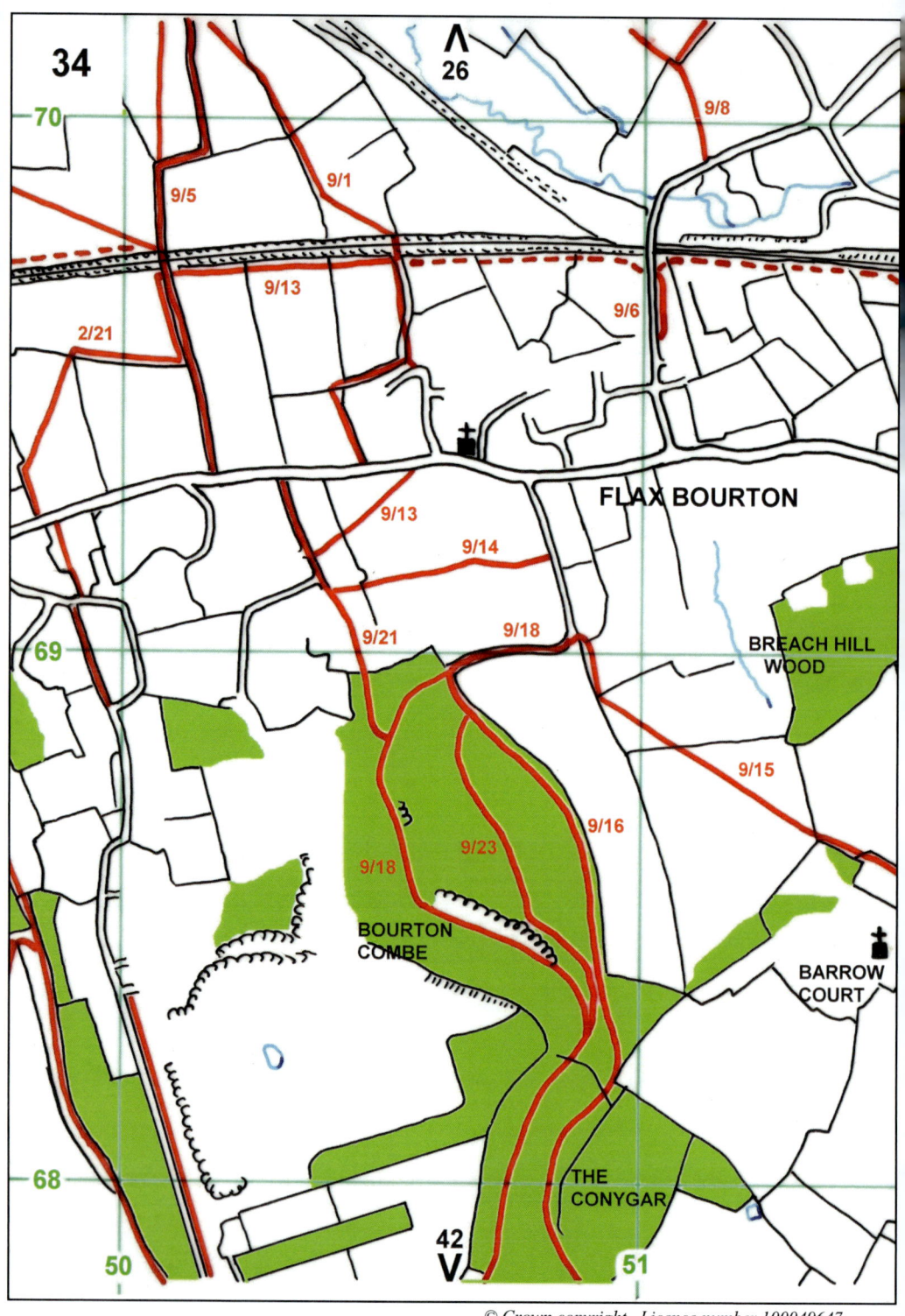

CAMBRIDGE BATCH

12/34
12/28
35
70
12/34
12/32
12/2
12/3
12/4
12/1
3/2
3/3
69
3/6
9/15
3/8
3/1
3/9
68
52
43
53
27

© Crown copyright. Licence number 100049647

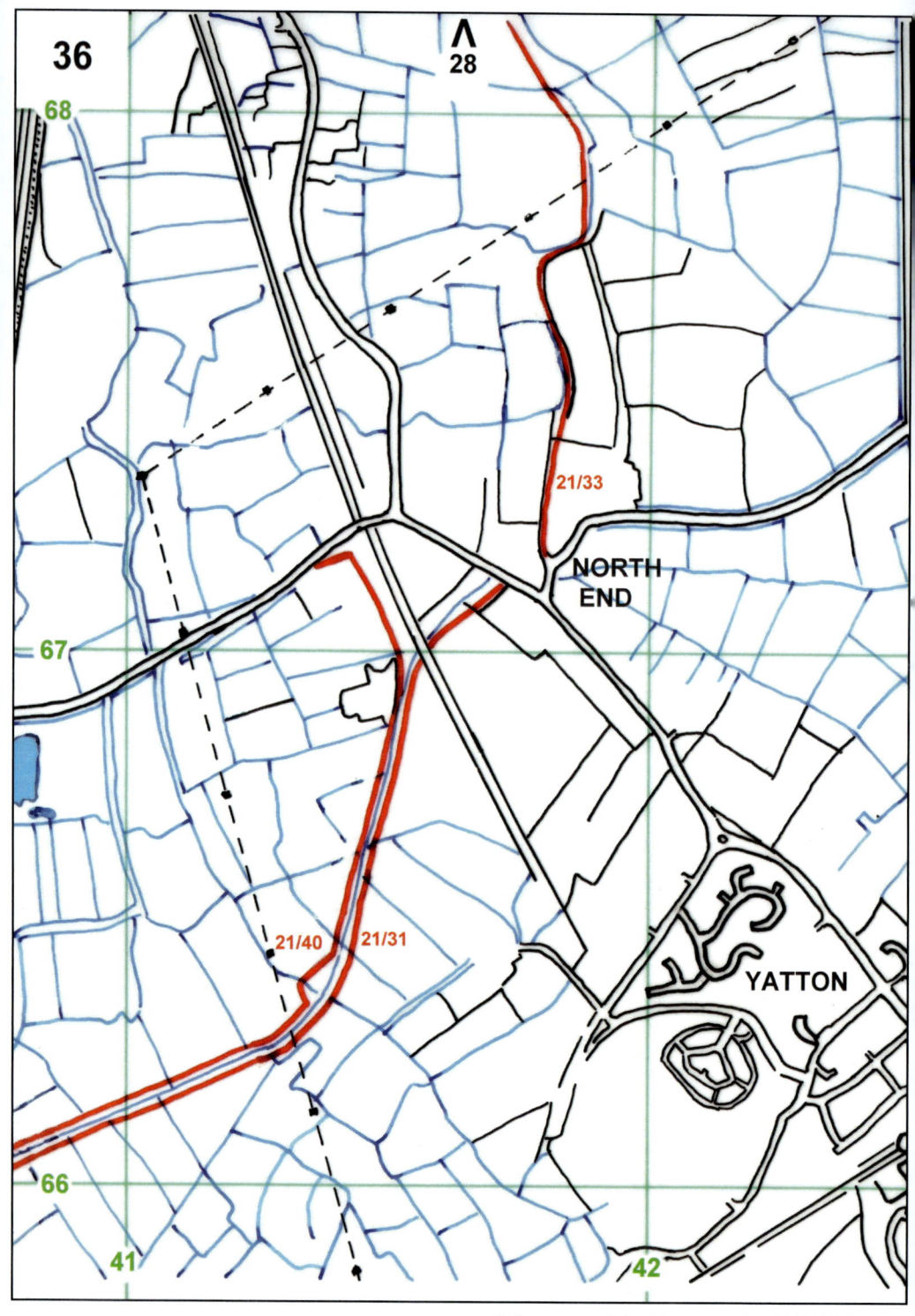

36

68

28

21/33

NORTH END

67

21/40  21/31

YATTON

66

41  42

© *Crown copyright. Licence number 100049647*

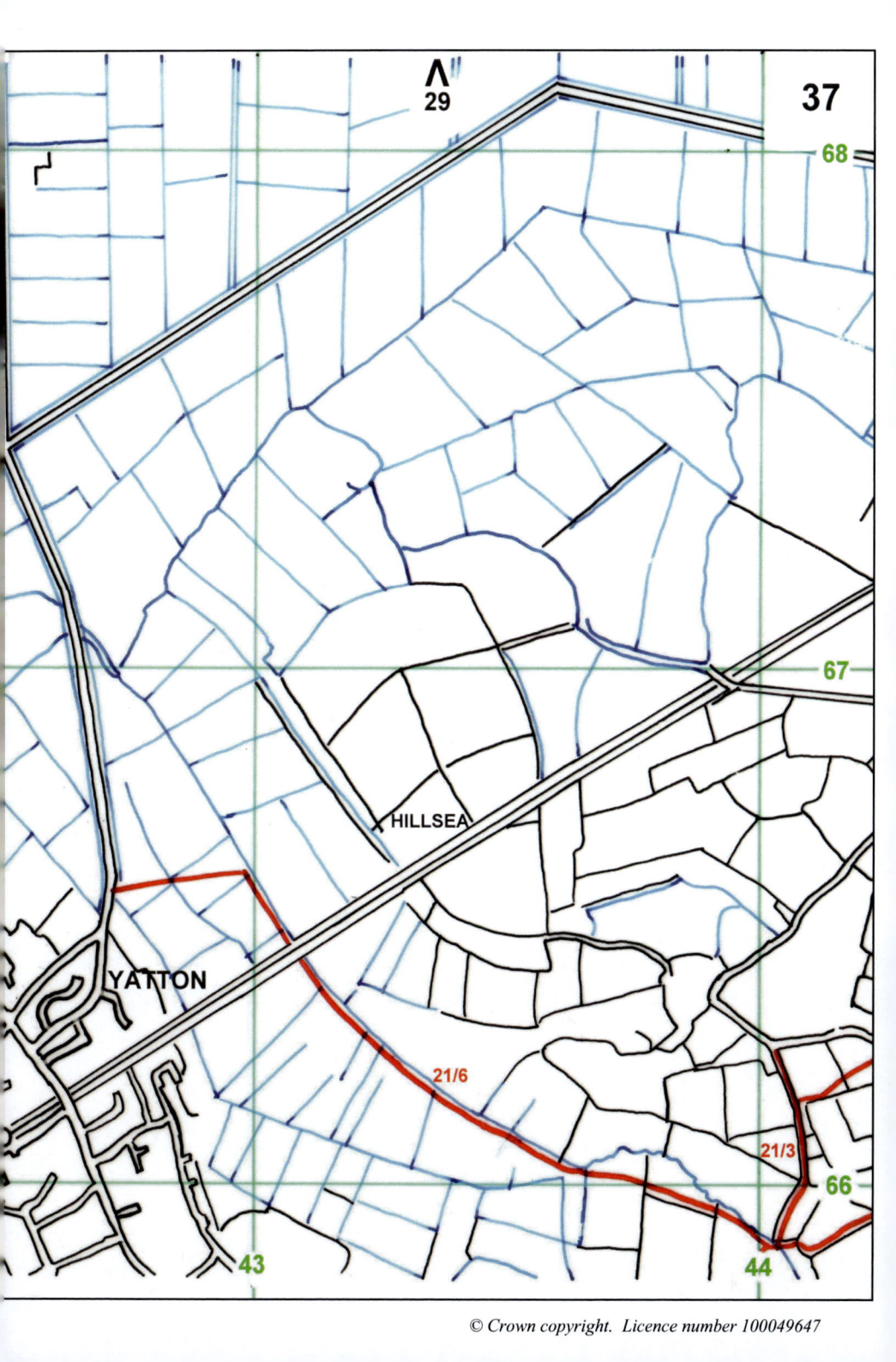

HILLSEA

YATTON

21/6

21/3

© Crown copyright. Licence number 100049647

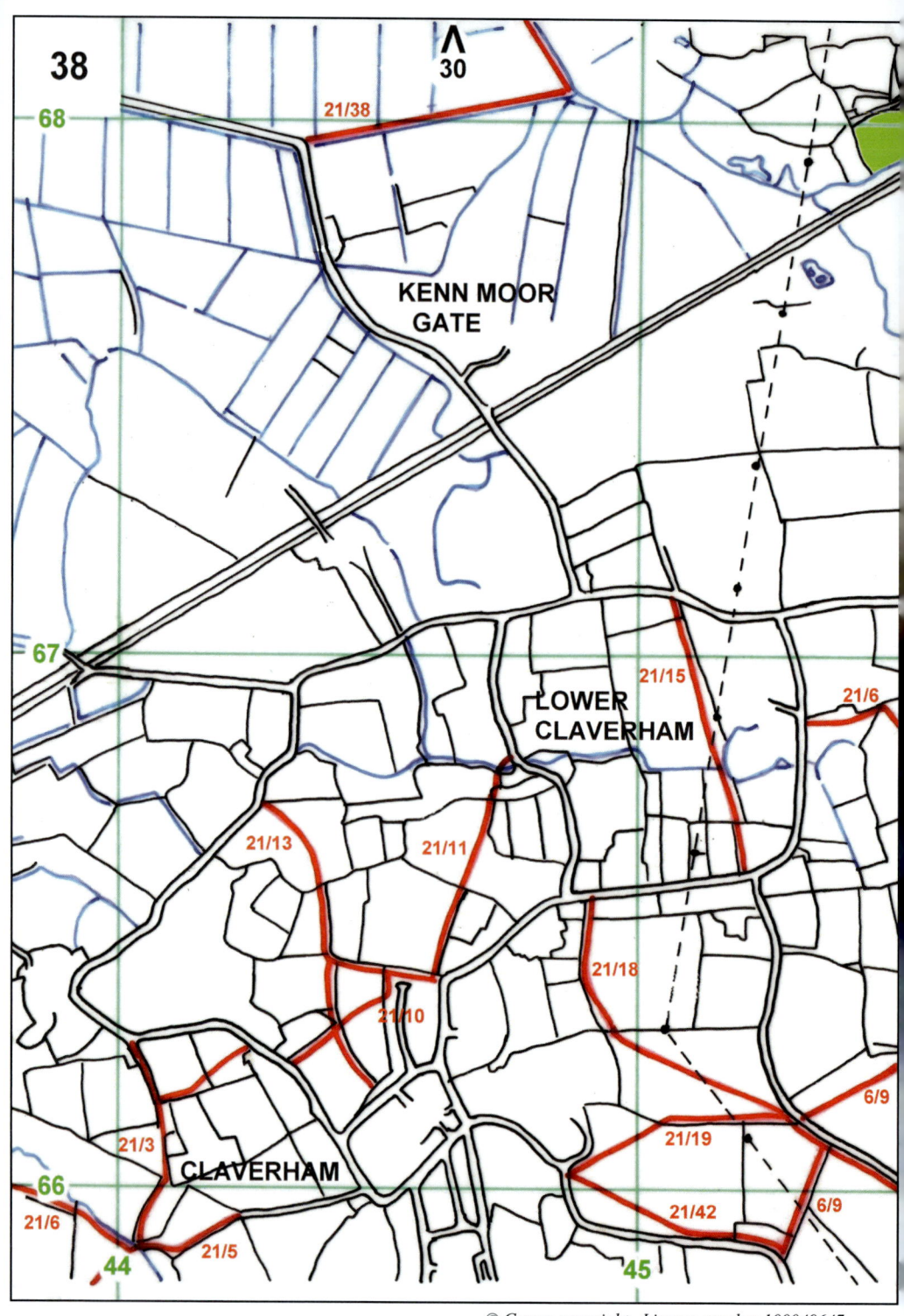

# 38

**KENN MOOR GATE**

**LOWER CLAVERHAM**

**CLAVERHAM**

21/38
21/15
21/6
21/13
21/11
21/10
21/18
6/9
21/3
21/19
21/6
21/5
21/42
6/9

© *Crown copyright. Licence number 100049647*

**39**

**BROCKLEY**

**CLEEVE**

**CLEEVE HILL**

4/6
4/6
4/6
6/9
4/4
4/3
6/9
9/10
6/12
6/13
6/12
6/11
6/10
6/10

31
68
67
66
46
47

© Crown copyright. Licence number 100049647

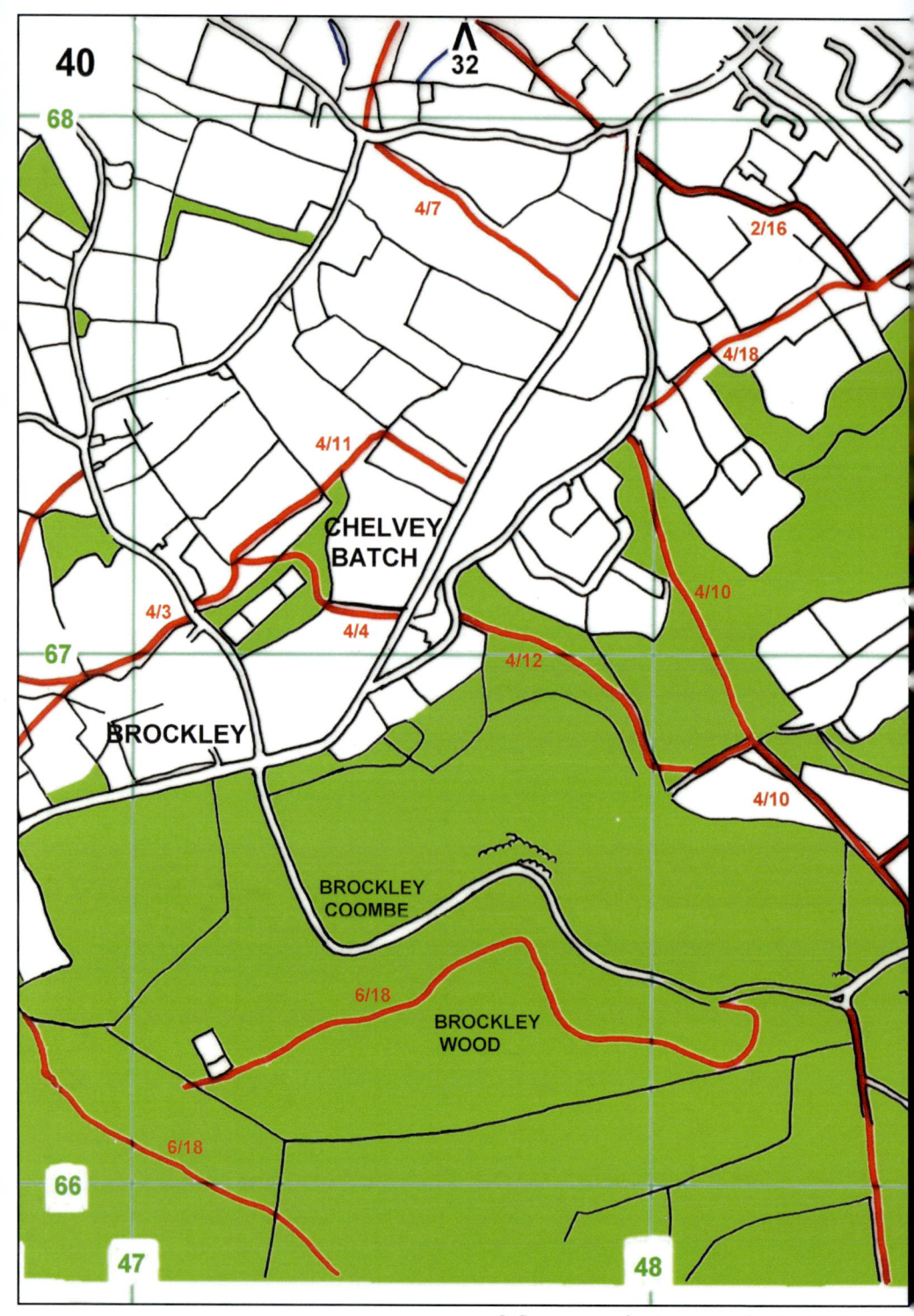

# 40

68

32

4/7

2/16

4/18

4/11

CHELVEY BATCH

4/3

4/4

4/10

67

BROCKLEY

4/12

4/10

BROCKLEY COOMBE

6/18

BROCKLEY WOOD

66

6/18

47

48

© Crown copyright. Licence number 100049647

**41**

JUBILEE STONE

2/5
2/7
2/8
2/13
2/14
2/8
2/57
2/18
2/8
21/19
21/19
2/18
2/38
HEALLS SCARS
2/45
2/44
2/37
2/46
2/48
2/17

DOWNSIDE

68
67
66
33
49
50

© Crown copyright. Licence number 100049647

# 42

JUBILEE STONE

THE CONYGAR

2/10
2/11
2/10
2/55
3/19
3/28
3/21
BARROW HILL
JUBILEE STONE
3/22

HYATT'S WOOD

2/51
2/47
2/29
2/40
2/51
2/38
2/44
2/47
2/39
2/38
OATFIELD WOOD
2/17
2/37
2/41

© Crown copyright. Licence number 100049647

**43**

Slade Wood
Batches Wood
Stevens Wood
Potters Hill
Felton

35
3/9
3/8
3/10
3/10
3/16
3/15
3/20
3/17
3/11
2/40
3/23
19/63
3/24
19/62

68
67
66
52
53

© Crown copyright. Licence number 100049647

## WALK 6   3 ½ miles

# Hannah More Road, Grove School, Youngwood Lane, South Common, Nurse Batch.
### *A fairly level and easy walk*

From Hannah More Road, opposite Scout hut, take walkway between Kingston Way and The Maples (east) to the T-junction then turn right to The Chimes. Turn right along The Chimes then cross to the far left corner and turn left on path to Church Lane.

Turn right along lane and then left in front of Church. Continue to Hairdressers on left and turn right on footpath crossing Whiteoak Way, then alongside school. On reaching sports ground path turn first left then right to continue in same direction.

At end of sports field path emerges into the open with views across to Backwell. Turn left here on bridle path through gap in hedge to next field then almost immediately right down some steps into enclosed section of bridleway. Again almost immediately turn right over stile and continue straight downhill, past pond and clump of trees on right, to gate and stile leading to Youngwood lane. Over stile and turn right along lane keeping a sharp lookout for any traffic.

After about ½ mile, at sharp right hand bend, go ahead into Cherry Orchard farmyard to far end and over gate. Follow hedge on left towards two gateways ahead. Continue through left gateway in same direction with hedge on right then over stile to road.

Turn right along road to T-junction then left along road for about ¼ mile to just past South Common Farm then over stile on right.

Bear slightly right across field towards small clump of young trees beyond which the ground slopes down. Turn left through gate immediately behind trees and continue downhill to gate into next small field.

Continue with hedge on right to stile and in same direction through fields to Nursebatch Farm.

At road turn right for about 100 yards then right again up farm drive. Continue over cattle grid and then turn left up hill along bridlepath. Keep field boundary to left through next two fields then where hedges form a Y follow hedge to left.

Continue in same direction in next field to stile. Over stile and head for far right corner and another stile. Straight across this narrow field and over another stile onto Rugby Club field.

Walk between pitches to end of railings on far side of field. Through gap in railings, turn left and follow through to stile at road.

Cross Engine Lane and continue straight ahead alongside allotments and Hannah More Park back to the start point

## WALK 7    5 ¼ miles

### Backwell Lake, Nailsea Ponds, Backwell Common.

*A fairly level walk crossing the railway line-and passing Chelvey Waterworks Pumping Station followed by a little climb partway up Backwell Hill. During a spell of wet weather, this walk can be rather muddy and waterlogged in places.*

From Backwell Lake Car Park, take left path round lake to Nature Reserve Board, turn left here through opening to path, go to top and turn Left at stone steps. Keeping hedge on your left follow footpath to Youngwood Lane. Turn left, walk about 1/2 mile along road take the 2$^{ND}$ stile on left (metal Post Footpath sign) go straight across field to opposite stile.

Over this stile and turn almost immediately left, over stile crossing rhyne, then right alongside rhyne to Railway Embankment. Go over stile and up slope. **Stop,Llook and Listen. If you hear or see a train, retreat back down slope until it has passed before carefully crossing lines** to stile opposite.

Follow footpath between Nailsea Ponds, over footbridge and continue straight across field to metal gate, cross next field to far right corner, cross plank footbridge go through gate, straight across next field to wooden gate, up over slope to the right corner Kissing Gate (also Metal farm gate). Take footpath straight across towards Pumping Station, cross double stile over brook, cross narrow field to Chelvey Lane.

Opposite and slightly left go through Kissing Gate then turn left and follow hedge up to corner, go slightly right across field heading for metal gate opening in stone wall on A370 just left of telegraph pole. Turn left and after 100 yards, cross over A370 into Chelvey Batch lane.

Up hill for 1/3 mile. Just past Chelvey Hollow turn left over stile (Bristol Water sign on gate) turn left and follow track to stile. Continue over 2 more stiles to Chelvey Farm.

Go through two gates close together, bear right through farm to gate, then kccp left along lane to Sores Court; at end bear slightly left and take Footpath on right. Go through 4 fields via stiles and gates leading to road.

Turn left to roundabout, then right along Church Lane past school on right, to sharp right bend. Turn left to the right of Coombe Cottage, and go along drive for <u>10 yards.</u>

Go Right over Stone stile, follow path for 75 yards. Over stile and continue below Church, parallel with houses, NE across field to large tree in far left corner. Take pathway between houses to emerge on Linmere Close, go slightly right heading for Church Lane.

Turn left down to Main A370. ***<u>Be careful here</u>***. Turn left, cross road, after few yards turn right over stile. Keeping hedge on right to stile in corner, go diagonally left across next field to stile: Again keep hedge on right down to next stile, go over, and then almost immediately left to next stile in corner.

Head towards railway arch, go under and follow track, go right and then left at bend, to road. Follow road back under railway line, under arch, take first footpath on right.

Cross this field towards houses to stile near wooden electricity pole. Turn right along path, then left on walkway below railway. Turn right under railway arch, over stile, cross drive, over another stile and bear left on to stile in corner of field.

Cross Station Road to Backwell Lake Car Park.

# WALK 8    2 ¾ miles

## Linear Park, Parish Brook, North Lane, Kingshill
### A short, level, field and town walk

From Clevedon Road car park turn left along Clevedon Road, pass Westway and Sunnymead Road. Just past Greenfield Crescent, turn left along surfaced path through the linear park. Continue past rear of schools and across footpath near children's play area.

Follow this main path as it continues through the linear park past another school on the right to reach a more open green area. Continue on central path to pass close by No.17 on your right.

After a few yards turn left at path T junction. Follow path through to road, cross road and continue for about 40 yards. Turn right at walkway through to Pound Lane. Cross road and turn right along road to first bus stop. Turn left down footpath to Godwin drive. Cross road and continue on footpath through to kissing gate and small field (it can be muddy for a while now).

Cross field to farm gate, through gate and continue towards pylon and another farm gate. Through gate and turn left to follow Parish Brook. Through kissing gate into next field and skirt around farm buildings to stile.

Follow Parish brook to another stile. Then turn left over next stile. Straight across field to stile opposite. Continue through to Causeway View.

Turn right along road to no through road on right. Turn right here through to The Causeway. Cross road with care to footpath on left to continue along Parish Brook for about 200 yards. Turn left over stone stile with small dog hole.

Bear sharp left go through gate and turn right to follow hedge up to drive. Continue along drive and right along North Lane and passage to North Street. Turn left and pass Fir Leaze and Queens Road. Take first left down Kingshill passing John Whitings Cottage (the oldest in Nailsea) on your right.

Turn right at junction and right again in front of corner shop.

Turn left up Chapel Barton alongside the Moorend Spout.

Continue along left side of Rock Avenue past Gilbeck Road and Lion Close. Turn left up footpath opposite No 9 through to Silver street. Turn right along Silver street past Beechwood Road and Camp View to reach footpath on left. Turn left down footpath to Westway.

Keep right along Westway back to Clevedon Road and turn right here back to the car park and the start point.

---

## *Also by Nailsea and District Footpath Group*

**THE NAILSEA ROUND** – **a 9 mile walk in the countryside around Nailsea and 6 shorter circular walks**

**THE INN THING** – **10 circular walks starting and finishing at local pubs.**

*Both books are available directly from the Group or local shops.*

## NAILSEA AND DISTRICT FOOTPATH GROUP

Formed in 1975, the principal aim of the Group was, and still is, to encourage people to walk the definitive Rights of Way in Nailsea and adjacent parishes; that is to enjoy the countryside. In so doing the Group has always contributed to the preservation, protection and maintenance of precious, often ancient footpaths so frequently under threat.

Our programme offers a range of whole day, part day, weekday and weekend walks of varying distances and degrees of difficulty. The walks range from 2 miles and very easy to 18 miles and strenuous. Many walks are local but we add interest and variety to the programme by including areas such as the Mendips, the Cotswolds, the Quantocks, the Welsh hills and Devon. To explore further afield we include short walking holidays in the UK and longer trips abroad. The programme is published on a six-monthly basis. Posters in local libraries and notice boards also advertise the walks.

The Group has about 150 members of varying abilities. We welcome and encourage new members of all ages. You may walk with the Group on two occasions before joining. We recommend that all walkers are equipped with waterproof walking footwear, appropriate clothing for seasonal weather and their own first aid kit. Our leaders can and will advise where necessary.

The membership fee is currently £4 per year. The group has third party indemnity insurance, but members need to insure privately for accidental injury.

## **WARNING**

## WALKING CAN SERIOUSLY IMPROVE YOUR HEALTH